For Fiona – J.Z.

First edition for the United States, Canada, and the Philippines published in 2004
by Barron's Educational Series, Inc.

Text copyright © Jonny Zucker 2004
Illustrations copyright © Jan Barger 2004

First published in Great Britain in 2004 by
Frances Lincoln Children's Books, 4 Torriano Mews,
Torriano Avenue, London NW5 2RZ
www.franceslincoln.com

All inquiries should be addressed to:
Barron's Educational Series, Inc.
250 Wireless Boulevard
Hauppauge, New York 11788
http://www.barronseduc.com

Library of Congress Catalog Card No.: 2004104911
International Standard Book No.: 0-7641-2671-7

Printed in Singapore
9 8 7 6 5 4 3 2 1

FESTIVAL TIME!

Fasting and Dates

A Ramadan and Eid-ul-Fitr Story

Jonny Zucker

Illustrated by Jan Barger

It's the first day of Ramadan –
the ninth month in our Islamic year.
We remember how Muhammad
began to receive the words
of the Qur'an from Allah.

My older brother won't eat
or drink from dawn to sunset
for the whole month.
I am too young to fast.

Tonight I'm eating a delicious sweet date. It's the first thing our Prophet Muhammad ate after he fasted.

We hear the call to prayer,
which tells us it's time
to go to the mosque.

It is the Night of Power when Allah
spoke the first words to Muhammad.
We pray and listen to the Qur'an,
which is read aloud.

We look at the shining new moon
and know that Ramadan is over
and our festival of Eid-ul-Fitr can begin.

We enjoy a delicious feast
with our family and friends to
celebrate our festival of Eid-ul-Fitr.

What are Ramadan and Eid-ul-Fitr about?

Every Muslim has five basic duties. These are called the Five Pillars of Islam. They are:

1. Faith in God. Muslims must declare that there is no God but Allah and that the Prophet Muhammad is his messenger.
2. Prayer. Muslims must pray five times a day.
3. Charity. All Muslims must give money to the needy (called **Zakat**).
4. Fasting. During Ramadan, Muslims fast from sunrise to sunset.
5. Pilgrimage. Once in a lifetime, Muslims are called on to make a pilgrimage (a religious journey) to Mecca, in Saudi Arabia, if possible.

Ramadan is a holy month. It was the month when the Prophet Muhammad received the first verses of the Qur'an (the Muslim holy text) from Allah. It is a time for reflection, for meditation, for carrying out additional prayers each evening, and for listening to the Qur'an being read in the mosque. The entire Qur'an is read by the time of the Night of Power, the last ten days of Ramadan. Fasting begins at daybreak and ends at sunset. This means that you cannot eat or drink during this time. Muhammad used to break his fast with a cup of water and a sweet date, which restored some of the energy he lost during the day. He would then pray before having the main evening meal.

Young children are not supposed to fast. People who are ill or on medication and people who are traveling are excused from fasting but should make up any lost days at a later date, or feed a needy person for each day missed. Fasting is a remembrance of Allah's commandments. It teaches patience, self-control, and charity, and it should not endanger your health.

Ramadan is a hard but blessed month, and its end is met with the joy and pleasure of Eid-ul-Fitr. During Eid-ul-Fitr, families visit each other, share a special meal, and participate in a feeling of sharing with others and in a sense of achievement. It is a special time for children, who are dressed up in new clothes and are given presents—there is a feeling of love and belonging. Eid-ul-Fitr is a celebration, a coming together, and a return to normal living after a period of personal reflection and spiritual renewal.